SUMMER ICE

Life along the Antarctic Peninsula

written and photo-illustrated by Bruce McMillan

Houghton Mifflin Company

Boston 1995

To Lauri

previous page photo: skuas on iceberg,
Bransfield Strait, King George Island, South Shetland Archipelago

facing page photo:
Anvers Island, Palmer Archipelago

Copyright © 1995 by Bruce McMillan

Designed by Bruce McMillan

Library of Congress Cataloging-in-Publication Data

McMillan, Bruce.
Summer ice: life along the Antarctic peninsula / Bruce McMillan
  p. cm.
  Includes bibliographical references, glossary, and index.
  ISBN 0-395-66561-2
  1. Natural history—Antarctica—Juvenile Literature. [1.
Natural History—Antarctica. 2. Antarctica.] I. Title
QH84.2.M38   1995   93-38831
508.98′9—dc20   CIP
                   AC

Printed in Singapore

TWP   10   9   8   7   6   5   4   3   2   1

It's like no place else.

Ice

Antarctica is an island continent so cold that some of it is covered by ice two miles thick. It's a desert of ice at the bottom of the world. Glacial ice, formed from snow that fell hundreds of thousands of years ago, flows as slow-motion rivers to the ocean. Along the coast, chunks of glaciers break off. Some are huge — as large as entire buildings and even whole towns. These icebergs float about in the Antarctic Ocean for years before they finally melt.

To exist, life needs water in liquid form, not solid ice. Even with twenty-four-hour sun in the summer, Antarctica is too cold and dry for most forms of life to survive.

However, there is a place on the continent where a few species of plants and animals thrive every summer. On some days the prevailing winds and currents "warm" the temperature to a few degrees above freezing. It snows, and even rains. This place is along the west coast and islands of the Antarctic Peninsula. It's the peninsula of land and ice that extends north from the continent toward South America.

Bransfield Strait

Land Plants

In frigid, barren Antarctica, the basic needs for plant growth are barely present. To grow, plants need three things: light, warmth, and nutrients. Not one tree exists anywhere in Antarctica.

But a few plants live along the peninsula. Where can they grow? The few areas not covered by ice are almost all rock. There is hardly any soil. So some plants grow on what exists everywhere here. They grow on the snow and ice. The summer sun warms exposed surfaces to provide life-sustaining meltwater.

Microscopic plant algae "bloom" on glaciers. Algae grow in such large quantities that some ice cliffs look like they're covered by a fine layer of red (or sometimes green) dust. However, it's living "plant dust."

red algae
Paradise Harbor, Antarctic Peninsula

red and green algae
Paradise Harbor, Antarctic Peninsula

red and green algae, young Weddell seal
Paradise Harbor, Antarctic Peninsula

moss-covered rocks, gentoo penguin colony
Cuverville Island, Errera Channel

moss (close-up)
Cuverville Island, Errera Channel

Plants don't grow only on ice here. Rock cliffs are colored in shades of yellow, orange, and brown. The colors are those of lichens, flat plants that stick to and grow on exposed rock. Lichens are actually combinations of two types of plants, algae and fungi, that grow as one. Together they are able to survive at lower light levels, colder temperatures, and a drier moisture content than they can tolerate separately. They grow slowly, some only half an inch (1.25 centimeters) in diameter in a hundred years. But they live for a very long time. Some Antarctic lichens still growing are older than the English language used to write this sentence.

At the "warm," northern end of the peninsula, only two types of hardy flowering plants, a grass and a flower, grow on what little sandy soil there is. Non-flowering plants, lush green mosses, form patches of color. Mosses create soft green carpets near bird colonies, where they thrive on the nutrient-rich fertilizer of guano.

Plant life may be limited on land, but there is a place here at the bottom of the world where plants flourish under the constant summer light. It's a place with some degree of warmth and large amounts of minerals and nutrient salts. It's a place where life-sustaining water is found year-round. It surrounds the peninsula and all of the continent. It is the Antarctic Ocean.

Marine Plants and Krill

The Antarctic Ocean is the stormiest ocean in the entire world. The winds and waves are ferocious, but those same winds and waves help stir up the ocean's minerals and nutrient salts. There are more nutrients in these waters than in any other ocean. With plenty of food, near-constant summer sunlight, and the warmth of water in liquid form, the ocean teems with vast amounts of tiny microscopic marine plants—plant plankton.

Plankton are named after the Greek word *planktos*, which means "drifting." They float freely in the ocean, drifting with the currents. Plant plankton are eaten by animal plankton. Both are in turn eaten by larger shrimplike animals—krill (*Euphausia* species). As krill swim through the sea, they guide plankton into their mouths with a sweeping motion of their front legs.

Krill are constant and speedy travelers. Their back legs paddle them forward faster than one foot (30.5 centimeters) per second. They never stop swimming, and that's quite a long workout considering that some adult krill may live five years. Since krill are heavier than water, they would sink to the bottom if they stopped swimming, and krill paddle-legs are built for swimming, not walking.

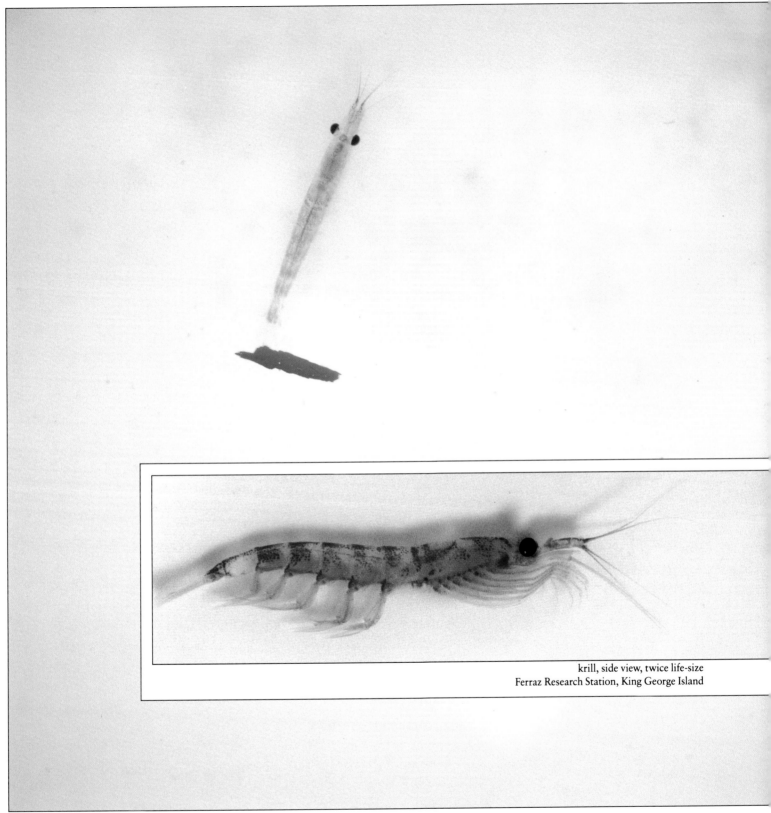

krill, top view, one-and-a-quarter life-size
Ferraz Research Station, King George Island

krill, side view, twice life-size
Ferraz Research Station, King George Island

krill, top view, life-size
Ferraz Research Station, King George Island

Krill travel in swarms throughout the Antarctic Ocean. They orient themselves to each other by using their biological light, which is like a firefly's light that stays on. The vast number of krill is almost unimaginable. The amount of water that fills a bathtub can have as many as 15,000 of these creatures swimming in it. Krill make the sea pink in places. The combined weight of all the krill in the Antarctic Ocean is greater than the combined weight of any other animal in the entire world.

That's a lot of krill, and those krill are a lot of food for larger animals. Squid eat krill. Fish eat krill. Just about all the animals in Antarctica eat krill. If they don't eat krill, they eat something that has already eaten krill. Krill is the major food source, and because it lives in the ocean, all other Antarctic animal life must live in or near the ocean, too. The largest animals in Antarctica — and also the largest in the world — feed on krill, and live here in the ocean. They are baleen whales.

humpback whale and calf
Admiralty Bay, King George Island, South Shetland Archipelago

Whales

Baleen whales eat massive amounts of krill. They gulp huge mouthfuls of seawater loaded with krill and a few small fish. They strain the water back out through their teeth, which hang down from the upper jaw like hairy-fringed plates, and are made of a substance called baleen, or whalebone.

One species of baleen whale that summers in the Antarctic Ocean is the humpback (*Megaptera novaeangliae*). Humpbacks eat nothing all winter when calving in waters far north of here. However, in the summer a single humpback swallows an estimated average of more than two million tiny krill each day.

How can these feeding whales swim among chunks of ice and stay warm? Their size and shape help. Large, torpedo-shaped bodies mean they have the least possible amount of skin exposed to the cold water. Also, they have lots of insulation—fatty blubber. But the blubber may hold in too much body heat. Even in the icy sea, whales sometimes need to cool down. They do this by adjusting the blood flow in their tails, fins, and flippers, where they have little blubber but many blood vessels. The vessels control the blood flow to these uninsulated parts in contact with the ocean, and either carry away excess internal heat or hold in body warmth.

a pair of humpback whales, one spouting
Bransfield Strait

humpback whale, breaching
Bransfield Strait

humpback whale, tail slapping
Bransfield Strait

male killer whale
Bransfield Strait

female killer whale
Bransfield Strait

16

Unlike the baleen whales, which migrate to warmer waters in winter, killer whales (*Orcinus orca*) stay in the Antarctic Ocean all year long. They travel in groups, or pods. Males are easily spotted by their tall, five-and-a-half-foot (180-centimeter) dorsal fins, much larger than the females' fins. Of all the predators of warm-blooded animals anywhere, killer whales are the largest. While baleen whales mostly eat krill in Antarctica, killer whales, toothed whales, eat the animals which have eaten krill: fish, squid, penguins, and seals.

Killer whales often work as a team during a hunt. When a pod of hungry whales finds a seal on an iceberg, they swim in a coordinated formation to create a large wave. The wave rocks the iceberg so the seal slides off into the water. The seal doesn't stand a chance. A crabeater seal can cruise as fast as 17 miles (27 kilometers) per hour, but hungry killer whales can sprint twice as fast at 34 miles (55 kilometers) per hour.

Seals
and
Fur Seals

Like whales, seals have plenty of insulation. Adults have a thick layer of fatty blubber that not only keeps them warm but provides them with energy reserves and buoyancy in the water. Antarctic seals have larger bodies than similar seals who live elsewhere. Newborn seal pups have a temporary fur pelt that keeps them warm on the ice until they're able to swim.

There are no crabs in Antarctica, but there are crabeater seals (*Lobodon carcinophagus*). Obviously, they don't eat crabs. They eat krill. The baleen whales here in the Antarctic Ocean eat an estimated 43 million tons of krill in a year. But crabeater seals eat even more—63 million tons. With that much food volume, there must be a lot of crabeater seals here. There are. More than half the seals in the entire world are crabeater seals, and they all live in Antarctica. They swim open-mouthed, sucking in krill. When a seal catches one, it pushes up its tongue and squirts the mouthful of water out its cheeks through specially shaped cheek-teeth that act as strainers. But crabeaters don't swallow their food until they have a whole mouthful of krill.

Crabeater seals rest on free-floating ice. They move awkwardly when out of the water, but of all the seals along the peninsula, crabeaters are "the fastest seals on ice." They lunge, bounce, and wriggle along as fast as 15 miles (27 kilometers) per hour.

crabeater seals
Argentine Islands

crabeater seal, resting on iceberg
Paradise Harbor, Antarctic Peninsula

crabeater seal, circling an ice floe
Argentine Islands

leopard seal, resting
Argentine Islands

leopard seal (left) and Weddell seal (right), both resting
Argentine Islands

Leopard seals (*Hydrurga leptonyx*) are krill seekers, too. They have similar specialized cheek-teeth for straining krill, their primary food here on the peninsula. But leopard seals also have large front teeth, powerful jaws, and serpentine necks for catching and eating something much bigger than krill. They are the only seals anywhere who regularly prey on birds and marine mammals. Usually the males eat penguins and seal pups of species not their own. They often leave permanent parallel tooth scars on crabeater pups that are fortunate enough to escape their fearsome jaws.

Adult Weddell seals (*Leptonychotes weddelli*) use their specialized teeth for chewing through ice to keep breathing holes open in the winter. But along the peninsula in the summer they don't have to chew. They can rest on ice floes. Weddells are not bothered by nearby leopard seals. If they were threatened, they might growl at the leopard seal. Weddells are the noisiest seals, especially underwater. When swimming, they "talk" to each other in songlike whistles, chirps, and trills that can sometimes be heard nearly 19 miles (30 kilometers) away.

Weddells usually make a series of eight- to fifteen-minute dives at about 1,000 feet (300 meters) to feed on squid and octopus. But they are able to dive to almost 2,000 feet (600 meters), and can stay underwater for over an hour — as long as 73 minutes. Weddells are among the best seal divers. Another kind of seal on the peninsula, though, can dive deeper than all the seals in the world.

Weddell seal, stretching
Cuverville Island, Errera Channel

The south elephant seal (*Mirounga leonina*), currently the champion seal diver, can stay underwater for about two hours and can dive over a mile deep—5,640 feet (1,720 meters). South elephant seals are also the largest of all the world's seals, at 600 to 1,200 pounds (270 to 540 kilograms). Like all the seals here, they come ashore to molt—to shed their skin and fur every summer. They visit the northernmost islands of the peninsula. Female south elephant seals bear their pups on land, usually farther north than the peninsula, while crabeater, leopard, and Weddell seals birth and nurse their pups on ice along the peninsula.

Unlike all of these seals, another species, the Antarctic fur seal (*Arctocephalus gazella*) is not a true seal. When swimming, fur seals use their front flippers to propel themselves; true seals use their tails. But all seals, including fur seals, belong to the suborder of mammals called Pinnipedia, which in Latin means wing (*pinna*) footed (*pedis*)—the wing-footed mammals.

Fur seals, true to the first part of their name, have more fur than the other seals who live here. How thick is it? People have about 100,000 hairs on their heads. A fur seal's protective outer fur and fine underfur—with about *300,000* hairs per square inch (47,000 per square centimeter)—is thick enough to trap a layer of tiny air bubbles. This layer of air keeps them warm and dry—even when swimming underwater.

Animals who live here must make their own heat, as warm-blooded marine mammals and birds do. It's too cold for animals such as amphibious frogs and reptilian turtles, which depend on the surrounding temperature for heat. However, there are several exceptions. A number of insects (and some fish) have their own internal biological antifreeze. Others keep from freezing by stealing heat from other animals. Tapeworms and a few insects, such as lice, live as parasites in and on seals and some birds. Imagine an elephant seal louse huddled in a pocket of air trapped in scaly skin while being squeezed by 30 atmospheres of pressure during deep seal dives. It must be quite a ride.

Antarctic fur seal, scratching and grooming
Melchior Islands, Dallmann Bay, Palmer Archipelago

Penguins

Penguins, like seals and whales, generate their own heat. Penguins, too, have blubber beneath their skin to keep them warm. As much as one-third of their weight can be a layer of insulating, energy-storing fat.

Since penguins are birds, they are covered with feathers. But their feathers, unlike any others, are extremely fine. At 70 per square inch (11 per square centimeter), they seem more like fur. Penguins shed their feathers every year at the end of summer. Their feathers are scattered over the rocks where they live.

But as penguins molt, they grow new feathers. Penguins are constantly preening. They maintain their feathers with an oil that is secreted at the base of their tail. They spread the oil by using their bills, and this waterproofs their feather suits. The cold ocean water never touches penguin skin. For even more insulation, a layer of air bubbles is trapped in their unique feathers. Penguins are so well insulated that when snow falls on their backs, it doesn't melt.

Ironically, keeping cool in this land of summer ice is a problem for penguins. They regulate their body heat by controlling the flow of blood to their flippers and feet. Excess body heat generated from an activity such as swimming escapes through the undersides of their flippers. They also adjust the flow of blood to their feet, just as whales do in their tails.

chinstrap penguins, resting on iceberg
Moon Bay, Livingston Island, South Shetland Archipelago

chinstrap penguins, porpoising
Bransfield Strait

chinstrap rookery
Half Moon Island, Moon Bay, South Shetland Archipelago

chinstrap penguins, parent and chick
Half Moon Island, South Shetland Archipelago

Unlike their parents, newborn penguin chicks don't have blubber insulation and waterproof feathers to keep them warm. Their nests, made out of rocks piled in a bowl shape, are exposed to the snow and wind. So chicks depend on their fluffy down feathers and their nesting parents' body warmth to protect them from the cold. Newborn chicks are rarely left uncovered; the parents take turns going to sea for food.

Chinstrap penguins (*Pygoscelis antarctica*) grow to stand 27 inches (68 centimeters) tall, but that still makes them the smallest of the three penguins that live along the peninsula. They swim as far as 20 miles (32 kilometers) from their rock nests to catch krill. Making relatively shallow one-and-a-half-minute dives, as deep as 200 feet (61 meters), they catch about sixteen krill per plunge. Chinstraps have to make many dives and catch hundreds of krill before they return to their chicks. Back at the nest, the chicks stick their heads into their parents' mouths to eat the partially digested krill that the parents regurgitate.

chinstrap penguins, parent feeding its chick
Half Moon Island, South Shetland Archipelago

All three species of brushtail penguins — chinstraps, Adélies, and southern gentoos — often stop to rest on icebergs during feeding trips. Adélies (*Pygoscelis adéliae*) travel the farthest to feed — as far as 30 miles (48 kilometers) — and dive to depths of 250 feet (76 meters), which is about 50 feet (15 meters) deeper than the chinstraps dive. Adélies are also the first penguins on the peninsula to lay their eggs. They live farther south than the other two brush-tails. The summer season is shorter there, so they start raising their young earlier. The chicks have to mature before winter.

The Antarctic Peninsula is as far north as Adélie penguins nest. Adélies and Emperor penguins (*Aptenodytes forsteri*), the largest of all the penguins, are the only species that nest south of here on the Antarctic continent.

Chinstraps and Adélies nest here in the summer, but they spend their winters farther out, on pack ice. In the winter the ocean surface freezes. Free-floating pack ice forms and surrounds all of Antarctica. By midwinter it covers more than half the Antarctic Ocean. The chinstraps and Adélies move out to where they can swim among the pack ice floes. But southern gentoos will stay, if it's a moderately "warm" winter.

Adélie penguin
Point Thomas, King George Island, South Shetland Archipelago

gentoo penguin, swimming
Admiralty Bay, King George Island, South Shetland Archipelago

gentoo penguin, diving
Cuverville Island, Errera Channel

Southern gentoos (*Pygoscelis papua elsworthii*), the largest of the brush-tails, live along the warmer, upper end of the peninsula. They have bright orange-red bills. Northern gentoos (*Pygoscelis papua papua*) live farther north, beyond Antarctica. Southern gentoos have smaller bills, flippers, and feet than their northern relatives. This helps to keep them warm because penguins lose heat through unfeathered, and therefore less insulated, parts of their body.

Of the peninsula's three species, southern gentoos can stay underwater the longest—as long as 2 minutes—and dive the deepest—to depths of more than 492 feet (150 meters). So they don't travel as far from their rookery as the other two species of brush-tails for food.

Penguins usually shake off after a swim. Yet they shake their heads at other times, too. It may look as if they have a cold and are shaking off a runny nose. The drips are not due to a cold; they are related to what the penguins drink. But what can a penguin drink? The fresh water here is locked up as ice. Like many seabirds, penguins drink the only liquid water that's available: the salty ocean water. They are able to do this because a pair of glands in their heads concentrate the salt. This brine then runs down their bills, and the penguins shake their heads to rid themselves of the brine drips.

gentoo penguin, shaking off after a swim
Cuverville Island, Errera Channel

Two sounds are common along the peninsula coastline: howling winds and penguin calls. Rookeries are noisy places. When one penguin starts calling, the call seems to spread until many penguin brays can be heard a half-mile away. Penguins call so that their mates can find them in a crowded rookery. They also call so that their chicks will come running at mealtime.

Since chinstraps and Adélies eat mostly krill, the rocks at their rookeries are covered in pink guano. Southern gentoos eat more squid and fish with their krill, so the guano around their nesting areas is a whiter shade of pink.

Penguins, colored in black and white, have something in common with almost all the other birds and marine mammals in Antarctica. From killer whales to gentoo penguins, these Antarctic animals are all primarily black and white. In this land of snow and ice, they all match the colors of their environment. Penguins' black backs and white bellies help camouflage them even more when swimming. The colors match the light sky above and the dark sea bottom below, protecting them from killer whales and leopard seals.

Penguins have little to fear on land here. Since there are no land mammals anywhere in Antarctica, there are no mammalian land predators. However, for unguarded eggs and chicks, danger usually lurks nearby in the form of predatory birds.

gentoo rookery, with young gray chick
Cuverville Island, Errera Channel

gentoo parent and older black-and-white chick
Port Lockroy, Weincke Island, Palmer Archipelago

Birds
of
Flight

Penguins are wary of skuas (*Catharacta* species). These gull-like predatory birds are always on the lookout to steal unguarded eggs or to attack chicks. They often work in pairs. While one distracts the adult penguin, the other goes after the unguarded egg or chick. Skuas have their own chicks to feed. Of the two types of skuas along the peninsula, both of which prey on fish and penguins, one eats more fish. But both types will attack the chicks and eat the eggs of almost any Antarctic bird.

White sheathbills (*Chionis alba*) roam freely through penguin rookeries. They are scavengers and eat almost anything — even penguin guano. Sheathbills also steal a meal by attacking and distracting penguins when they are feeding their chicks. The interrupted feeding means a regurgitated krill spill for themselves.

There is an abundance of birds along the peninsula, and in all of Antarctica. The combined weight of all birds in Antarctica — most of them penguins — is greater than the combined weight of all the Antarctic seals and whales. But of course, the combined weight of all the krill is even greater.

white sheathbill, wandering near a chinstrap rookery
Half Moon Island, Moon Bay, South Shetland Archipelago

a pair of skuas, near a gentoo rookery
Cuverville Island, Errera Channel

kelp gull
Bransfield Strait

limpet shells, regurgitated by kelp gulls
Half Moon Island, South Shetland Archipelago

Antarctic limpets (*Nacella concinna*) are shellfish that survive the winter by migrating. They summer in the shallow water, then move out into deeper water for the winter.

In the summer, limpets are easy picking for the only species of gull in Antarctica. A scattering of empty limpet shells means a breeding colony of kelp gulls (*Larus dominicanus*) is nearby. Kelp gulls, also called southern great black-backed gulls, may feed near the ocean's kelp but they don't actually eat it. They eat limpets. When the tide is out, they go wading, plucking limpets from the shallow waters and swallowing them whole, shell and all. Later, after digesting the edible part, they regurgitate the indigestible shells.

Some birds of flight stay on the Antarctic peninsula all year, while others migrate far north for the winter. Flocks of cape petrels (*Daption capense*) never leave, but some of the kelp gulls travel up to South America. South polar skuas (*Catharacta maccormicki*) migrate as far north as Greenland, at the top of the world.

Cape petrels
Drake Passage

blue-eyed shags, adults and mature chicks at nesting colony
Paradise Harbor cliff, Antarctic Peninsula

blue-eyed shag
Waterboat Point, Paradise Harbor, Antarctic Peninsula

Antarctic blue-eyed shags (*Phalacrocorax atriceps bransfieldensis*) stay all year. Summer is the time when they raise their young. Finding nesting material on the barren peninsula can be a problem. Blue-eyed shags collect mosses, lichens, seaweeds, and anything else they can find to make their nests, and glue it together with their wet guano. The cliffs below their nests are covered with white guano. Majestic wings that spread to 49 inches (124 centimeters) fly them to sea, where they dive into the water—as deep as 100 feet (30 meters)—for fish. Sometimes when they return with a meal for their young, skuas attack them and nab the dropped fish for themselves.

Antarctic terns (*Sterna vittata*) look like Arctic terns (*Sterna paradisaea*), which only summer here to feed. Antarctic terns live here all year, nesting and raising their chicks in the summer. They catch Antarctic silverfish (*Pleuragramma antarcticum*), and like so many animals here, they also feed on krill. When Arctic terns leave for the polar north at the end of summer, Antarctic terns stay to fatten up their tiny bodies for winter survival. They may need the extra energy to shiver. Since tern feathers are typical bird feathers, similar even to the feathers of tropical birds, terns aren't well insulated like penguins. It appears that these tiny birds generate some heat in the winter through muscle activity while at rest. They exercise without going anywhere—they shiver.

Antarctic tern, holding its catch of an Antarctic silverfish
Paradise Harbor, Antarctic Peninsula

Winter

All Antarctic life survives the frigid winters unique to this part of the world in one of two ways. It either adapts to the cold, or it migrates to a warmer climate, even if only to the edge of the pack ice.

Every winter the temperature along the peninsula, the warmest part of Antarctica, drops to between + 17 and − 4 degrees Fahrenheit (− 8 and − 20 degrees Celsius). Winds blow regularly at over 100 miles (161 kilometers) per hour. In midwinter, the sun appears in the sky for a few hours, but only on the upper half of the peninsula. The bottom half, closer to the continent, is dark. Pack ice covers much of the ocean. The land of summer ice becomes a land of winter ice. It's like no place else on earth.

Antarctica

the bottom of the world

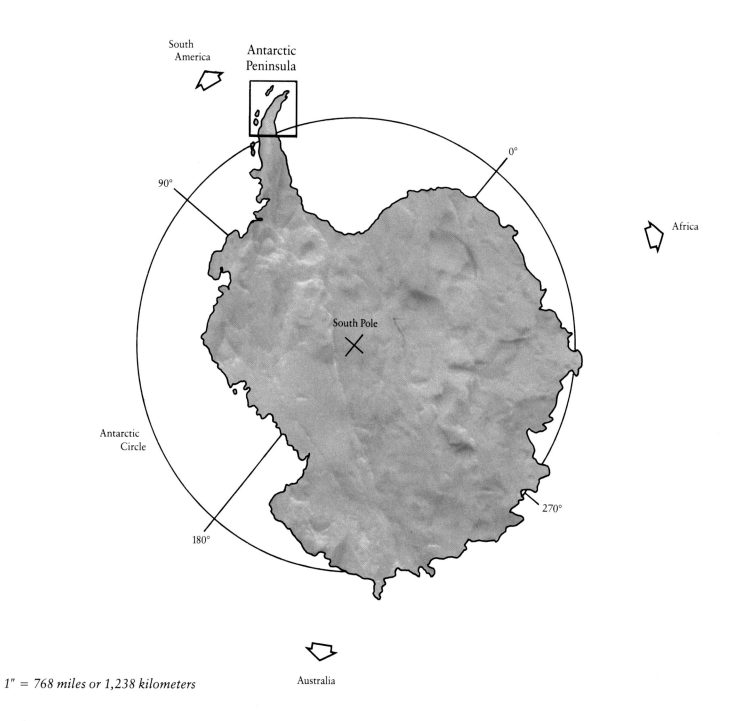

South
America

Antarctic
Peninsula

0°

90°

Africa

South Pole

Antarctic
Circle

270°

180°

1" = 768 miles or 1,238 kilometers

Australia

The Antarctic Peninsula

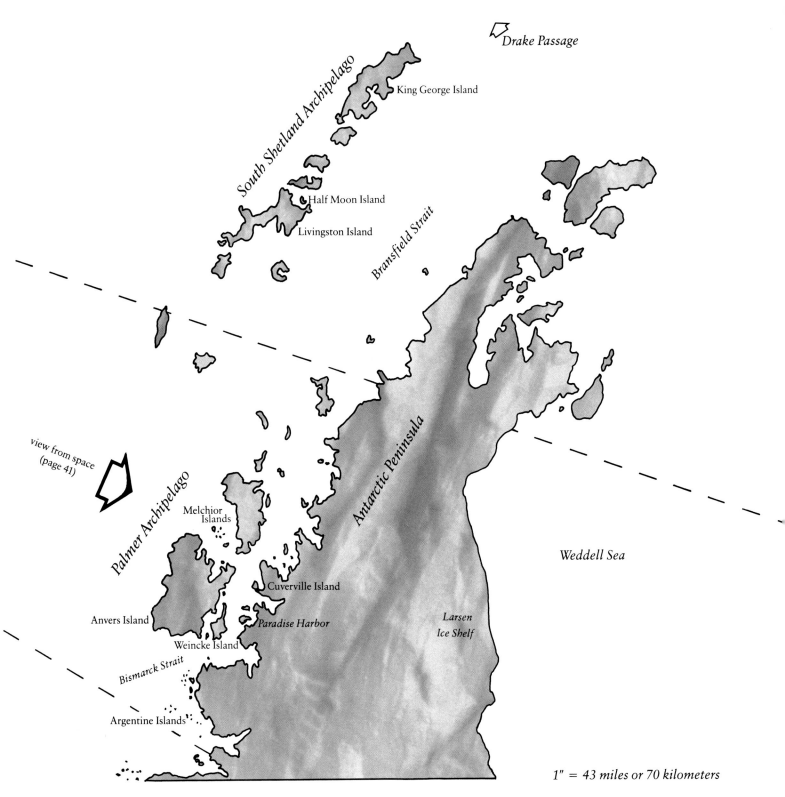

Drake Passage

South Shetland Archipelago

King George Island

Half Moon Island

Livingston Island

Bransfield Strait

view from space
(page 41)

Palmer Archipelago

Melchior
Islands

Anvers Island

Cuverville Island

Paradise Harbor

Weincke Island

Antarctic Peninsula

Weddell Sea

Larsen
Ice Shelf

Bismarck Strait

Argentine Islands

1" = 43 miles or 70 kilometers

Glossary

Algae—small plants, sometimes one cell, that live in damp places and use sunlight, carbon dioxide, and water to make their food.

Baleen—the substance that hangs from the roofs of some whale mouths as filterlike plates, used to strain food from expelled seawater. Also called whalebone, it is made from keratin, the same matter as fingernails.

Baleen Whales—the whales of the suborder Mysticeti that have baleen for capturing their food.

Biological Antifreeze—chemicals made within a living organism which prevent ice from forming, therefore lowering the organism's freezing point.

Blubber—fat deposits beneath the skin of whales, seals, and penguins which prevent heat from escaping and act as energy (food) reserves.

Brine—water with a high concentration of salt.

Brush-tail—the long, pointed penguin tail composed of stiff feathers, which is longer than that of all other penguins and is unique to the genus of *Pygoscelis* penguins: Adélies, chinstraps, and gentoos. Also a name for a penguin of that genus or group.

Buoyancy—the ability to float.

Calving—the birthing of a newborn from the mother cow.

Cold-blooded—refers to those animals that regulate their body temperatures by exchanging heat with their surroundings, thus making them dependent on the surrounding environment for body heat. Also called ectothermic.

Crabeater—the common name for the seal *Lobodon carcinophagus*. The name was originated by seal hunters in the 1800s, who mistakenly thought that the seals were eating crabs when they were actually eating krill.

Dorsal Fin—the top central fin on whales, which is used to maintain balance when swimming.

Earflaps—the small, external furry flaps on fur seal heads next to their ear holes.

Flippers—the paired limbs of whales, seals, or penguins, which are wide and flat for propelling and/or steering when swimming.

Fungi—the plants that do not contain chlorophyll, thus do not need light to grow.

Fur Seals—the sea mammals belonging to the subfamily Arctocephalinae that have earflaps and thicker fur than true seals. They use their front limbs to prop themselves up on land, and use their tails to steer underwater.

Glacier—a huge mass of ice formed from compacted snow that flows like a slow-motion river over a land mass.

Guano—the nitrogen excrement of penguins and birds, which is also food (fertilizer) for plants.

Ice Floe—a small flat expanse of floating ice, a large portion of which is visible above water.

Iceberg—a massive floating body of ice broken off from a glacier, with only an approximate ten percent visible above water.

Insulation—a barrier which prevents the transfer of heat.

Kelp—long brown seaweed found in relatively shallow waters and floating as tall vertical plants attached to the sea bottom.

Migrate—to change living locations on a seasonal basis.

Molt—to shed a worn outer covering while growing a new covering.

Nutrient Salts—sources of plant nourishment, such as phosphates, nitrates, and potassium, that are found dissolved in the Antarctic Ocean.

Pack Ice—floating ice that has been driven together to form a single mass; develops on the ocean surface around Antarctica in the winter.

Pelt—the fur and skin of an animal.

Peninsula—a projection of land which extends out from a land mass and into a body of water.

Plankton—tiny plant or animal organisms that live near the surface of a body of water and drift with its currents.

Pod—a group of same-species marine mammals that travel together.

Predator—an organism that preys on other organisms as a food source.

Preen—the bird activity of using the bill to groom its feathers.

Prey—the live animal food source for a predator.

Regurgitate—to cast partially digested food back up one's throat.

Rookery—the nesting area for a group of penguins. Also called a colony.

Scavenger—an animal that feeds on dead or decaying matter, or steals a meal from another animal.

Toothed Whales—the whales of the suborder Odontoceti, which have teeth for grasping their prey.

True Seals—the sea mammals belonging to the family Phocidae, which do not have earflaps. They use their back limbs (tails) to propel themselves underwater, and use their front flippers to steer.

Warm-blooded—refers to those animals, including humans, that regulate their body temperature by generating their own heat, usually to a temperature higher than their surroundings. Also called endothermic.

Bibliography

Ashworth, William. *Penguins, Puffins, and Auks: Their Lives and Behavior.* New York: Crown, 1993.

Boner, W. Nigel. *The Natural History of Seals.* New York: Facts on File, 1990.

Campbell, David G. *The Crystal Desert: Summers in Antarctica.* Boston: Houghton Mifflin, 1992.

Chester, Jonathan. *Antarctica: Beauty in the Extreme.* Philadelphia: Running Press, 1991.

Cousteau, Jacques-Yves, and Yves Paccalet. *Jacques Cousteau: Whales.* New York: Harry N. Abrams, 1988.

Davenport, John. *Animal Life at Low Temperature.* London: Chapman & Hall, 1992.

Dunbar, M. J. *Ecological Development in Polar Regions: A Study in Evolution.* Englewood Cliffs, N. J.: Prentice-Hall, 1968.

Galimberti, Diana. *Antarctica: An Introductory Guide.* Buenos Aires: Zagier and Urruty Publications, 1991.

King, Judith E. *Seals of the World.* 2nd ed. Ithaca, N. Y.: Cornell University Press, 1993.

Laws, Richard M., and B. J. Le Boeuf, eds. *Elephant Seals: Population, Ecology, Behavior, and Physiology.* Berkeley: University of California Press, 1994.

Martin, Dr. Anthony R., et al. *The Illustrated Encyclopedia of Whales and Dolphins.* New York: Portland House, 1990.

May, John. *The Greenpeace Book of Antarctica.* New York: Doubleday, 1989.

McMillan, Bruce. *Penguins at Home: Gentoos of Antarctica.* Boston: Houghton Mifflin, 1993.

Moss, Sanford. *Natural History of the Antarctic Peninsula.* New York: Columbia University Press, 1988.

Nowak, Ronald M. *Walker's Mammals of the World.* 5th ed. Baltimore: Johns Hopkins University Press, 1991.

Parmelee, David F., and William J. L. Sladen. *Conservation of Antarctic Birds.* NSF-90-100. Washington, D.C.: National Science Foundation.

Parmelee, David Freeland. *Antarctic Birds: Ecological and Behavioral Approaches.* Minneapolis: University of Minnesota Press, 1992.

Riedman, Marianne. *The Pinnipeds: Seals, Sea Lions, and Walruses.* Berkeley: University of California Press, 1990.

Simpson, George Gaylord. *Penguins: Past and Present, Here and There.* New Haven: Yale University Press, 1976.

Stewart, John. *Antarctica: An Encyclopedia.* Vols. I and II. Jefferson, N. C.: McFarland and Company, 1990.

Stonehouse, Bernard. *North Pole, South Pole.* London: Multimedia Books Limited, 1990.

Trivelpiece, Susan G., and Wayne Z. Trivelpiece. "Antarctica's Well-bred Penguins." *Natural History.* December 1989: 29–36.

Watson, George E. *Birds of the Antarctic and Sub-Antarctic.* Washington, D.C.: American Geophysical Union, 1975.

A Note from the Author

Antarctica was called New South Iceland by seal hunters in the 1800s. But throughout Western history, and prior to its discovery in the 1800s, Antarctica has been referred to as Terra Australis Incognita (the unknown southern land). Long ago, the Greeks theorized the existence of Antarctica. They believed the world to spin around a fixed point. A constellation in the northern sky, Arctos (the bear), revolved around this point. They called the theoretical land area below it Arktikos (the Arctic), and they supposed an imaginary pole (the North Pole) as its axis point and named it Arctos after the constellation. The bottom end of this imaginary pole was logically referred to as "anti (opposite) Arctos" and, it may be inferred, the land at the bottom was "anti Arktikos"—Antarctica.

Antarctica's name may have been a second thought for the ancient Greeks, but when it comes to the coldest places on earth, Antarctica easily ranks first. Surprisingly, it is colder at the bottom of the world than at the top. This has to do with the fact that the top of the world is an ocean surrounded by land masses: Asia, North America, Europe, and Greenland. But the bottom of the world is a land mass, Antarctica, surrounded by an ocean. In the north polar region the Arctic Ocean moderates the temperature. In the winter, it gets colder on the land masses surrounding the North Pole than at the pole itself. But nowhere does it get as cold as at the bottom of the world. Antarctica, with its mountainous land mass, is higher in altitude and therefore even colder. Also, the white continent reflects more of the sun's solar radiation (heat) back into space. All of these factors make Antarctica the coldest place on earth. However, I found that the summer temperatures along the peninsula, often above freezing, were quite comfortable, especially with the long hours of daylight.

This book was photographed on the Antarctic Peninsula and its west coast islands during the Antarctic summer, in January and February, 1992. Travel aboard the MV Illiria and its zodiacs was coordinated and provided in part by Travel Dynamics, New York, New York. The only photograph not taken by me, the one of the peninsula on page 41, was taken from space by an astronaut aboard the NASA space shuttle *Discovery*. It was taken in 1991 during the September 12–18 flight, which was late winter in the southern hemisphere. The photo and information were provided through NASA, Houston, Texas, and the U.S.G.S. EROS Data Center, Sioux Falls, South Dakota. I am also indebted to Mr. Phan, a scientist at the Brazilian Ferraz Research Station, King George Island, for his help in making it possible to photograph the krill he was studying.

The photographs were taken with a Nikon F4/MF23 and FE2 with 24, 50, 180, and 300 mm AF Nikkor lenses, sometimes with a circular polarizing filter, and sometimes mounted on a Bogen Professional 3001/3025 tripod. The film used was Kodachrome 64 processed by Kodalux. The photograph taken from space was shot with a Hasselblad.

Index

Algae, 6, 9, 44
  green, 6
  red, 6
Antarctic limpets, 37
Antarctic Ocean, 4, 9, 10, 13, 14, 17,
    18, 28, 41, 45
  animal life, 13
  nutrients, 10
Antarctic Peninsula, 4, 6, 18, 28, 32,
    40, 43
Antarctica, 4, 28, 40, 42
  animals, 13, 17, 18, 32, 34, 37, 40
  naming of, 47
  plants, 6
  temperature, 4, 40

Biological antifreeze, 22, 44
Birds, *see also* Penguins, 22, 34–39
  Antarctic blue-eyed shag, 38, 39
  Antarctic tern, 39
  Arctic tern, 39
  Cape petrel, 37
  feathers, 39
  kelp gull, 37
  parasites, 22
  shivering, 39
  skua, 34, 37, 39
    south polar, 37
  white sheathbill, 34
Blubber, *see* Insulation, Penguins, Seals,
    Whales

Climate, 4, 8, 40
Cold
  survival, 22, 40
Cold-blooded, 22, 44

Fish, 13, 22
  Antarctic silverfish, 39
  food source, 14, 17, 32, 34, 39
Fungi, 8, 44

Glacier, 4, 6, 44
Guano, 8, 32, 39, 44
  food source, 34

Human
  hair, 22
  warm-blooded, 45

Ice, 4, 6, 31, 40
  glacial, 4, 44
  icebergs, 4, 14, 17, 24, 28, 45
  ice floes, 21, 28, 45
  pack ice, 28, 40, 45
Insects, 22
Insulation, 45

Kelp, 37, 45
Kelp gull, 37
Krill, 10, 13, 34
  behavior, 10
  biological light, 13
  combined Antarctic weight, 34
  description, 10
  food source, 13, 14, 17, 18, 21, 27,
    32, 39, 44
  number, 13
  weight, 10, 13, 34

Lichens, 9, 39

Marine mammals, 21, 22, 32
Migration, 40, 45
  Arctic tern, 39
  kelp gull, 37
  limpet, 37
  south polar skua, 37
  whale, 17
Moss, 9, 39

Penguins, 24–38
  Adélie species, 28
    behavior, 28, 31, 32
    chicks, 28
    blubber, 24
    body temperature, 24
    brush-tail species, 28, 31, 44

chicks, 27, 32
chinstrap species, 27, 28, 44
  behavior, 27
  color, 32
  drinking, 31
Emperor penguin species, 28
  feathers, 24
  flippers, 24, 44
gentoo, northern, species, 31
gentoo, southern, species, 28, 31, 32
  behavior, 31, 32
  body temperature, 31
  food, 32
  size, 31
  guano, 32
  insulation, 24
  molting, 24, 45
  nests, 27
  preening, 24, 45
  rookery, 26, 28, 32, 34, 45
  size, 27, 31
Peninsula, 4, 45
Plants, 6, 9, 10, 44, 45
  land, 6, 9
  marine, 10
  moss, 9, 39
  nourishment, 9, 45
  plankton, 10, 45
  soil, 6, 9
Predator, 17, 32, 34, 45
Prey, 17, 21, 34

Rain, 4

Seals, 18–24, 44, 45
  Antarctic fur species, 22, 44
    earflaps, 44
    fur, 22
  birthing, 22
  blubber, 18
  combined Antarctic weight, 34
  crabeater species, 18, 22, 44
    crabs, 18, 44
    krill, 18, 44
    population, 18
    pups, 21, 22, 45

prey, 21, 45
  speed, 17, 18
  teeth, 18
ear holes, 44
flippers, 22, 44
fur, 18, 22, 44
insulation, 18
leopard species, 20, 21
molt, 22, 45
parasites, 22
Pinnipedia, 22
pups, 18, 22
size, 22
south elephant species, 22
true seals, 22, 45
Weddell species, 21, 22
Snow, 4, 6, 24, 27, 32, 44
South America, 4, 37
Squid, 13, 17, 21, 32
Summer, 4, 6, 8, 10, 14, 21, 22, 24, 28,
    37, 39, 40

Trees, 6

Warm-blooded, 17, 22, 45
Water
  drinking, 31
  meltwater, 6
Whales, 13–18, 44, 45
  baleen (whalebone), 14, 44
  blubber, 14, 44
  body temperature, 14, 24, 45
  calving, 14, 44
  combined Antarctic weight, 34
  feeding, 14, 18
  flippers, 44
  humpback species, 14, 18
  killer species, 17, 32
    behavior, 17
    dorsal fin, 17, 44
    toothed, 17, 45
  pod, 17, 45
  size, 13
Wind, 4, 10, 32
  speed, 40
Winter, 28, 40

King George Island, South Shetland Archipelago